Big Cats
of the World

LEVEL  READER

Written by Kathryn Knight
Illustrated by Edizioni Larus S.p.A.

African Lion

The lion is the largest cat in Africa. It lives in grassy areas called the *savanna*. Lions live in groups called *prides*. The males take care of the pride. If an enemy gets too close—ROAR!!

Only the male lion has a thick mane. He sleeps about twenty hours a day and often hunts in groups at night. Lions hunt large animals, such as zebras and buffalo.

When it's very hot, lions rest in the shade or near water. Sometimes they nap on tree branches.

Baby lions are called cubs. Mother lions take care of their cubs for two years. The cubs learn the rules of the pride and how to hunt.

Cheetah

This graceful cat is the cheetah. It is one of the fastest animals in the world. It can sprint as fast as a car going 70 mph on the highway! Cheetahs can zigzag as they run, so it's hard for even a quick gazelle to escape a cheetah.

A mother cheetah may have two or three cubs
at a time. Before she hunts, she hides her cubs
in the thick grass. When the cubs are older,
the mother teaches them how to hunt. At one
year old, young cheetahs can take care of
themselves. They set out alone
on the savanna.

Look at the handsome coat of this big cat. The leopard's spots help it to blend in and hide in a forest or high grass. Leopards live in Africa and in southern Asia.

Leopards are good climbers. They often perch in a tree, looking for *prey* (animal for food).

Leopards hunt many different animals. A leopard is so strong, it can lift a heavy animal into a tree just by using its teeth.

Black Panther

A black panther is really… a leopard! Its spots are hard to see because its coat is so dark. Black leopards are able to hide in the shadows of a jungle or forest. A yellow leopard mother can give birth to both yellow and black cubs.

Asian Lion

There are not many lions left in the country of India. They live in a special park where they are safe from hunters. These are Asian lions, which differ from African lions in several ways. They have lighter-colored fur, they hunt smaller prey, and males and females live apart.

Bengal Tiger

Tigers have striped coats that help them hide in tall grass. The Bengal tiger of India and south-central Asia is called the "royal tiger." Males can weigh up to 600 pounds.

There are very few Bengal tigers left in the world. New laws help to protect this amazing animal.

A mother
Bengal tiger
can have three
cubs at a time. Cubs
stay with their mother for two years and
then go out on their own.

The Bengal tiger is so strong, it can hunt
animals much bigger than itself. It hunts deer,
pigs, and buffalo.

Snow Leopard

The snow leopard of Asia is a large cat that lives in high mountain areas. It has a thick, warm coat of fur and large, padded feet—perfect for its cold, snowy home.

Snow leopards are great hunters. They can make 50-foot leaps to catch large birds and mammals of all sizes.

Clouded Leopard

Clouded leopards also live in Asia. They are smaller than snow leopards. They weigh 35 to 50 pounds. Clouded leopards live in forests. By eleven weeks old, the cubs are already excellent tree climbers.

Have you ever seen the long teeth on pictures of saber-toothed tigers that lived long ago? Well, the teeth of a clouded leopard look a lot like those teeth!

Siberian Tiger

The Siberian tiger of northern Asia is the largest cat in the world. It can weigh 700 pounds—more than three average men! It is a powerful and quick hunter. There are not many of these beautiful tigers left in the wild.

The Siberian tiger likes to live alone in low mountain areas. It hides in forests and high reeds near rivers.

It eats large animals like wild pigs, deer, and elk. This tiger will even attack bears! It can carry a 300-pound animal and swim with it across a river.

Lynx

The lynx is the largest wild cat in Europe. It has tufts on its ears and a short tail. It lives hidden in dense forest areas. It is a skilled tree climber and can swim across rivers.

The lynx can attack with a lightning-fast sprint and leap as far as 16 feet! When it walks, it keeps its claws pulled in, so it does not leave clear tracks.

The coat of the Canadian lynx is thick and long. In the winter, the color is lighter, making the lynx hard to see against the snow. The Canadian lynx is a quick hunter. It can catch birds right out of the air!

Canadian lynx cubs are cute balls of fluff born in the spring.

Bobcat

The bobcat of North America is sometimes called a "red lynx." It has a sharp cry, and when it's in danger, it makes a sound like a cough. The bobcat is *nocturnal*—it hunts at night and sleeps during the day. Its favorite prey is a jackrabbit.

Ocelot

The ocelot (**ah**-suh-lot) of Central and South America is sometimes called a "painted leopard"—but it is not a leopard. It is a small wild cat that hunts at night.

Ocelot cubs look and act just like kittens. Cubs raised by humans will purr like house cats.

Jaguar

The jaguar is the largest cat of the Americas. It can weigh up to 265 pounds. It moves easily and quickly through the rainforest and is an excellent climber and swimmer.

Cubs stay with their mother until they are two years old. They learn the secrets of hunting, such as how to find turtle eggs, catch crabs and fish in the swamps, and how to chase monkeys without falling from the treetops.

The jaguar hunts for deer, large rodents, fish, and reptiles. With a great leap, the jaguar pounces on its prey, bites its neck, and drags it

Puma

Pumas live in North and South America, in cold mountains and in hot deserts, too. They may have tan coats, red coats, or yellow-gray coats. They weigh 75 to 240 pounds.

The puma is a strong hunter. It can leap 25 feet! Pumas will travel far in search of food—sometimes as much as 25 miles in one night.

North American Puma (Cougar)

Pumas in North America are called cougars, mountain lions, or panthers. The cubs are born with spots, which they lose after ten months.

Cougars will hunt for small and large prey. They eat mice, porcupines, birds, and foxes. Sometimes cougars attack livestock, like sheep. But most of the time, cougars stay away from farms and people.

Cougar cubs are often born in a cave in the summer. The mother protects them and keeps them clean by licking them.

A cougar can act just like a really big pet cat. It washes its face with a paw, rolls onto its back, and eats like a house cat. But, no matter how cute these cats may look, they can never be pets. These big cats are wild!